AF480638

When God Was Already There

by Brian Scoggins

Table of Contents

Prologue

A few weeks before the wreck, an unnamable stirring began to rise within our home — a whisper in the stillness I couldn't grasp at the time. It crept in quietly, without warning or explanation. The kind of presence you only recognize in hindsight, when you realize God had been speaking all along, patiently waiting for us to listen.

We were a family of six: Katie was 19. Meagan was 17. Donna was 15. Michael was 9.

Each of them carried their own light, their own rhythm, their own place in our home. I didn't know then that those ages would become sacred markers — frozen in time by what was coming.

One evening, Michael came to us with his small frame trembling, tears streaming down his cheeks. He was never one to cry easily, so seeing him that vulnerable sent a cold shiver through my heart. His voice quivered as he whispered that he felt like he was going to die. Not someday. Not eventually. Soon. Then he looked up at us with those innocent eyes and asked what we would do if he died.

We tried to wrap him in the reassurance every parent reaches for. We told him he was young, that he had his whole life ahead of him, that he wasn't going anywhere. But his gaze held steady, searching for a truth deeper than our comforting words.

"What would you do if I died?" His insistence sliced through the air, tightening something deep inside my chest.

We finally told him the truth — that we wouldn't want to breathe without him, that losing him would shatter us in ways we couldn't imagine. As we spoke, his eyes held a clarity, an innocence too pure for the weight of the moment.

"But why?" he asked softly, as if sharing a secret. "I would be with Jesus."

There was no fear in his tone. No tremor of doubt. Just the unwavering faith of a child who somehow understood more than we did.

In that moment, I was lost — unable to grasp the significance of his certainty. I didn't know then that God was already preparing us… already preparing him… for the storm ahead.

A few weeks later, it happened again. Late one night, as the glow of the computer screen lit the room, Michael came to me with tears spilling down his cheeks. His face was ashen, each breath shaky with dread. He told me he'd had a dream — a dream that he died. He described it with haunting detail: a car, a gray truck, and the moment when life faded from his eyes.

I tried to soothe him, to dismiss it as just a dream, but the fear radiating from him was unmistakable — like a cold draft seeping into my bones. The way he described it felt less like imagination and more like something he had witnessed.

And then, on the morning of the wreck, the vehicle that struck them was a gray eighteen-wheeler hauling coal.

In that moment, I failed to connect the pieces. I couldn't see the pattern unfolding. I didn't recognize the signs — the warnings threaded through our days like whispers from the divine. But now, looking back, it all becomes clear.

God was already there. God was already speaking. God was already preparing us for something we could never have braced ourselves for.

These moments weren't coincidences. They were holy threads, woven gently into the fabric of our lives, leading us toward the moment everything would change forever.

"And it shall come to pass afterward, that I will pour out my spirit upon all flesh; and your sons and your daughters shall prophesy, your old men shall dream dreams, your young men shall see visions." **— Joel 2:28 KJV**

Chapter One — The Morning Everything Changed

I got up early for work that morning, same as always. The house was still dark, quiet in the way only early mornings can be. Michael was asleep in the old red recliner, curled up the way he liked, his small body sinking into the worn cushion.

I walked over to him. "I love you, buddy," I said.

His eyes barely opened. "I love you too, Dad."

Those were the last words we ever spoke to each other.

I headed for the door, and that's when it hit me — a pull, sharp and sudden, telling me to stay. Call in. Turn around. Don't leave this house. It wasn't logic. It wasn't laziness. It was something deeper, something I couldn't name but could feel pressing against my chest like a hand trying to hold me in place. God's second warning. The first had come the night before the drive to my mother's house — words I spoke to my wife that surfaced from somewhere I didn't understand.

I went anyway.

At work, a heaviness settled over me that I couldn't shake. Something was wrong. I could feel it in my bones, in the pit of my stomach, in the way the air seemed too thick to breathe. I glanced at the clock. 7:40 a.m. That time seared itself into my mind — burned there, permanent, like a brand I'll carry the rest of my life.

A deputy walked past the meat case where I was working. He didn't stop, didn't say a word to me, but the sight of him sent a jolt of unease through my body that I couldn't explain.

Around 9:30, the phone rang. My wife's voice was a scream — raw and broken, the kind of sound that doesn't come from the throat but from somewhere deeper, somewhere that only opens when the worst thing you can imagine has just become real. I couldn't make out the words. I told her I was on my way.

The phone rang again.

"He's gone."

I asked who.

"Michael. He's gone. There was a wreck... he didn't make it."

She told me to meet her at the UAB Emergency Room in Birmingham. The girls were there. I needed to come now.

The drive didn't feel real. The world outside the windshield kept turning — cars moved, lights changed, people walked — but inside me, everything was collapsing. Pressure built in my chest like something was trying to crack me open from the inside. Part of me believed it was a mistake. Part of me was already breaking.

At the hospital, I was lost. Disoriented. Couldn't think straight, couldn't find where I was supposed to go. A friend who worked there met me outside and guided me to the ER. Before I could go in, there was chaos — and it happened fast.

A deputy told me I couldn't go to the wreck scene. Michael was still there. He hadn't been transported to Cooper Green yet. My boy was still out there, and they were telling me I couldn't go to him. I argued. I pushed. I demanded. My aunt wanted to come with us to see

Meagan, but something inside me said no. While I was going back and forth with the deputies, I learned what had hit them — an eighteen-wheeler carrying coal.

When I finally walked down that hallway toward the room, fear and hope tangled together inside me. A fragile, desperate hope — the kind you grip with both hands even when your knuckles are white and your arms are shaking. Maybe it wasn't as bad as they said. Maybe there was still a chance.

The door opened, and I saw Meagan.

Hope shattered. I felt the exact second it died — not gradually, not gently, but all at once, like glass hitting concrete. I remember seeing her eyes open. My wife remembers them closed. I don't know which memory is true. Time stretched, slowed, froze. The air in that room felt unnaturally cold, heavy with something sacred and terrible at the same time.

I prayed. "Father in heaven, take care of her. She is with You now."

Later that night, before Donna went into surgery, we were in the ICU with Katie when the phone rang. Cooper Green needed someone to come identify Michael. My wife couldn't do it — she was entering a rheumatoid flare, her body failing her at the worst possible moment. I was terrified. I didn't know if I could bear it. My stepdad volunteered to go.

Sometimes I regret letting him. Sometimes I don't. My last memory of Michael is rubbing his head, telling him I loved him. That memory is pure, untouched, whole. Nothing has corrupted it. Nothing ever will.

At some point, someone called asking about donating Meagan's organs. Anger rose fast — hot, blinding, instant. Then I heard on the news that a third child had passed. This was before Donna was even moved to ICU. The report was retracted. But Donna did pass and was revived. In that small hospital room, surrounded by machines and grief and the smell of antiseptic, they told me Meagan didn't make it either.

But deep down, I already knew.

"The LORD is nigh unto them that are of a broken heart; and saveth such as be of a contrite spirit." — Psalm 34:18 KJV

Chapter Two — The Room Where Heaven Met Earth

After they told us about Meagan, the world went quiet. Not peaceful — empty. Like all the sound had been pulled out of the room and replaced with a weight I could feel pressing down on my shoulders, my chest, the back of my skull.

A male nurse asked if we wanted to see her. He explained that we weren't allowed to touch her — it was still under investigation. I asked my pastor and my wife to be with us. The nurse led us down the hallway to the ER.

There she was. My beautiful seventeen-year-old daughter. Her eyes were still open, still full of life, as if she might blink at any moment and ask why we were all standing there crying. Her hair was covered in tiny fragments of glass that caught the light like something fragile and wrong. Even in death, she was still beautiful.

We prayed. We whispered, we cried, our voices trembling and breaking over every word. Then something came over me — a force I didn't summon, didn't control. I began to pray in tongues. The words poured out from somewhere beyond my understanding, beyond my grief, beyond the walls of that room. "Lord, do what I can no longer do. Take care of my daughter."

My wife reached toward Meagan's hair, wanting to touch her, to smooth it back the way a mother does. I reminded her — we weren't allowed. She pulled her hand back, and the pain of that small denial was almost worse than everything else.

Our prayers grew louder. Our crying grew heavier. Then the male nurse — tears streaming down his own face — stepped closer and said, "It's okay... you can touch her."

I don't know how long we stayed in that room. Time had no meaning. Minutes could have been hours. But the presence of Jesus was real, close, steady — as tangible as the cold air, as certain as the grief. That room became sacred ground. Heaven bent low and met us there, in the worst moment of our lives, and held us when we couldn't hold ourselves.

"Yea, though I walk through the valley of the shadow of death, I will fear no evil: for thou art with me; thy rod and thy staff they comfort me." — Psalm 23:4 KJV

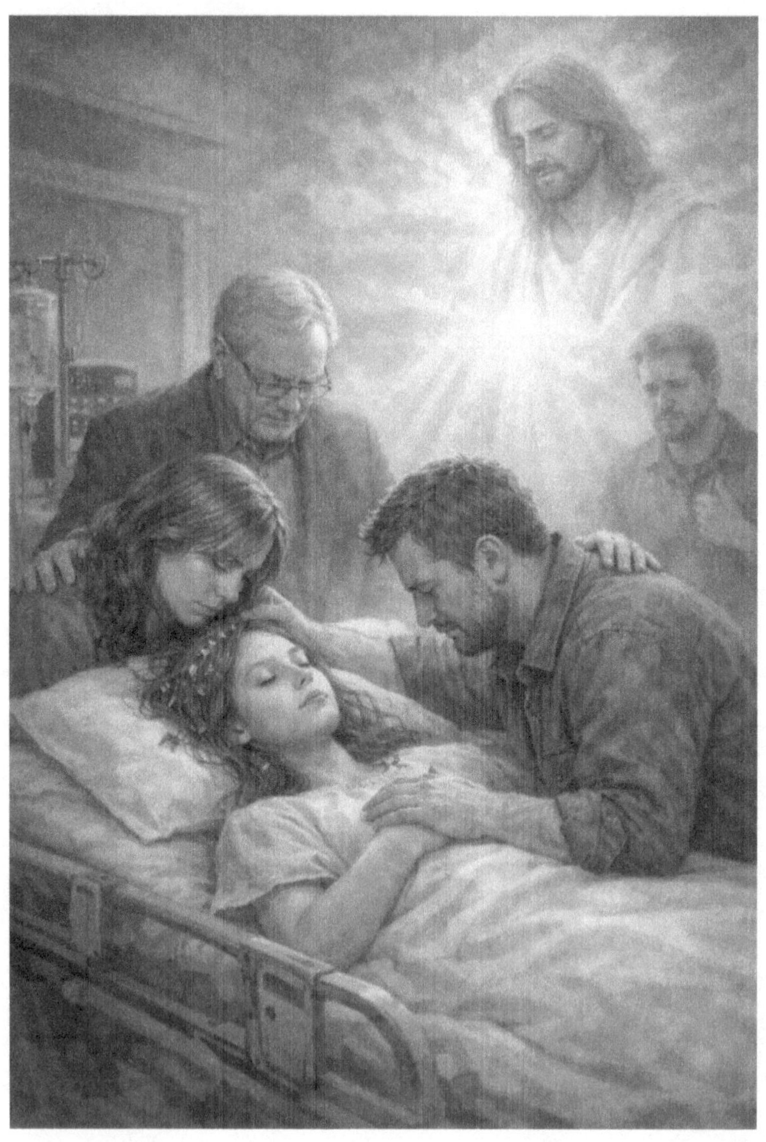

Chapter Three — Holding On to the Living

After leaving Meagan's room, someone said the words that pulled me forward when every part of me wanted to collapse: focus on the two still alive.

I called my mother. She and my stepdad were on their way to Florida — the whole reason we were staying at her house to watch the dogs. When I told her, she screamed. "Not Meagan!" The sound of her voice broke something in me all over again.

The phone wouldn't stop ringing. Every call was another voice, another cry, another person trying to find us, reach us, help us. We made our way to the ICU.

Katie, my oldest at nineteen, had the least injuries — bruised, shaken, but awake. She was alive, and the small relief of seeing her conscious was immediately tangled with guilt and fear. Relief felt wrong when two of my children were already gone.

Donna was fifteen and unconscious. Machines were breathing for her. She had a dissected aorta and needed emergency heart surgery. The surgeon came out to the lobby, which was full of family, friends, and church members — people who had dropped everything to be there.

My wife prayed for the surgeon right there in that lobby, out loud, in front of everyone. I watched the surgeon's face as she prayed. I don't know what he was thinking, but I saw something shift in his expression — something that told me medicine and faith had just met in the same space, and neither one flinched.

The surgeon walked back to the OR. Then came the hours. Hours of waiting — fear, hope, exhaustion, and prayer all twisted together into something that doesn't have a name. We had already lost two children. The thought of losing another was more than I could hold. So I prayed. We all prayed. And we waited.

"Fear thou not; for I am with thee: be not dismayed; for I am thy God: I will strengthen thee; yea, I will help thee; yea, I will uphold thee with the right hand of my righteousness." — Isaiah 41:10 KJV

Chapter Four — The Day Before Everything Changed

Before I go further, I need to take you back. Back to February 12, 2017 — the day before the wreck. The day God gave His first warning, and I didn't fully understand it.

My mom's house never felt like home. It was unfamiliar — I always felt like a guest there, sleeping in someone else's space, living out of bags. We were only there because we had to be. She and my stepdad were headed to Florida, and someone needed to watch the dogs. I had to be up for work at four in the morning, and the thought of spending the whole week there sat wrong in my chest.

That night, Michael came into the kitchen and asked for a piece of Angel Food Cake. I cut him a slice and watched his eyes light up — that simple, pure joy a child gets from something so small. We stood there together in the quiet of the kitchen, yellow light overhead, and I didn't know it would be our last real moment. Just cake.

Just a quiet exchange. Just a father and his son in a kitchen that wasn't theirs.

Meagan wasn't home yet — she was out with her boyfriend. I never saw her that night. I didn't realize it was the last chance I'd ever have.

My wife and I had argued all day about whether to spend the week at my mother's house. I wanted to stay home and drive over each day to check on the dogs. She wanted to stay there. By evening, the argument had left us both ragged. Around eight o'clock, she gathered the kids and said she was going — with or without me. We only had one vehicle. Her words were final.

I lingered outside, the chill biting my skin, a weight pressing on my chest that I couldn't explain. Then words slipped out of my mouth — words I didn't plan, didn't rehearse, didn't even fully understand: "I don't know how or why, but one day you're going to regret this."

I wasn't trying to hurt her. The words surfaced from somewhere deeper than anger — somewhere I believe now was God Himself. His first warning. A whisper disguised as frustration, planted in my mouth before I knew what it meant.

So I went. I followed them to my mother's house. I carried a heaviness I couldn't explain — a sense that something was shifting, that something was coming. I just didn't know what.

"Trust in the LORD with all thine heart; and lean not unto thine own understanding. In all thy ways acknowledge him, and he shall direct thy paths." — Proverbs 3:5-6 KJV

Chapter Five — How the Wreck Happened

I wasn't there when the wreck happened. Everything I know comes from investigators, medics, witnesses, and from my daughters—Katie and Donna—the only two who survived. What follows is the truth as it was told to me, a father searching for the last minutes of his children's lives.

After I left for work that morning, the kids got up around 7 a.m. and got ready for school with my wife. It was an ordinary morning. They weren't running late, they weren't rushing—they would have made it to class before the bell. Nothing about the day hinted at what was coming.

Katie, my oldest daughter, was driving. Meagan was in the passenger seat. Michael and Donna were in the back. They followed their usual route, the same one if we were at my moms house, a path that included an intersection everyone in our area knows is dangerous. The layout of that intersection almost dares drivers to change lanes while crossing—something that should never happen. Add in a hill, a blind spot, and fast-moving traffic, and you have a place where a single miscalculation can turn deadly.

When they reached the intersection, Katie did exactly what she was supposed to do. She stopped at the yield light, being overly cautious. She looked. She waited. She made sure nothing was coming. She saw a truck at the top of the hill—at least 150 to 200 yards away. Far enough that any reasonable driver would have expected to have time to slow down. Far enough that she should have been safe.

She made her turn. She was already out of the main road and onto the road she was turning onto.

But the truck wasn't slowing down.

The driver of that eighteen-wheeler—a gray truck hauling coal—wasn't even close to the speed limit. Investigators told us later he was going 83 miles per hour in a 45. He wasn't just speeding. He was flying.

As he crested the hill, he changed lanes inside the intersection—right where the road design tempts drivers to do it. Only this time, it wasn't a small mistake. It was a fatal one.

He hit their car with such force that after the impact, he still managed to continue uphill for about 80 yards. Their car was thrown into a parked eighteen-wheeler trailer sitting at least 30 feet away. The violence of that impact is something I still struggle to comprehend.

Katie witnessed things no child should ever have to see. She remembers the moment of impact, the sound, the chaos in the car. She remembers trying to make sense of what had just happened while her siblings screamed, while metal groaned and glass shattered around them. She remembers reaching for Donna in the backseat, calling out for Meagan and Michael, her mind desperate to find them in the confusion and pain.

Katie didn't know, in those first chaotic moments, what was happening around her. As she sat there hearing sirens and the frantic voices of EMTs trying to reach them, with blood everywhere and her mind struggling to make sense of anything, she had no way of knowing that Michael was pinned beneath Meagan's seat in the floorboard. She didn't know he was crying out that it hurt, reaching toward Donna, calling her name. She didn't know that the sounds Meagan was making beside her weren't words at all—just painful, broken noises that didn't sound human and didn't make sense to her terrified mind.

What none of my children knew in those moments was that the driver of the eighteen-wheeler never came to check on them. He stayed by his truck, watching from a distance while strangers ran toward the wreckage to help. The people who stopped—ordinary men and women on their way to work—were the ones who tried to reach my children, who called out to them, who did everything they could while waiting for the medics to arrive.

Donna would later share something that still shakes me. When the lawyers spoke with her after she regained consciousness, they showed her a series of photos. Without hesitation, she pointed to the driver of the eighteen-wheeler. She shouldn't have been able to do that—not with the injuries she had, not with the chaos she'd been pulled from—but she recognized him instantly. For a long time after that, I couldn't wear a solid white shirt again. That's what he had been wearing, and the moment Donna saw that color, it brought everything back to her. She wanted people to know what she saw, and I honor that by telling it here.

Donna's memories are fractured—just flashes of noise, the weight of the seatbelt pinning her, the world spinning outside the window. She remembers the sirens, the strangers' voices, the cold air rushing in where the windows had been.

Everything else comes from others: the investigators' timelines, the medics' careful words, the stories of people who stopped to help. I have tried to piece it all together, moment by moment, to understand those final minutes. But there is only so much a father can know—only so much anyone can bear to carry.

What I do know is that lives can change in a heartbeat. And that morning, for my family, everything did.

"God is our refuge and strength, a very present help in trouble." — Psalm 46:1 KJV

Chapter Six — When Donna Woke Up

I don't remember the exact day. Everything after the funeral bled together — one long, shapeless stretch of pain. I was broken in every way a person can be broken. It was sometime after we buried Michael and Meagan, and Donna had been unconscious since the wreck.

Her body had survived a dissected aorta for an entire day before they could get her into surgery. The doctors called it a miracle, and I believed them, because nothing about Donna's survival made medical sense. Machines did her breathing. Every day we sat at her bedside, praying, watching the monitors, begging God for one more sign that she was still in there.

Then her eyes fluttered open.

The news rippled through the family like electricity. We rushed to her side, crowding around the bed, afraid to breathe too hard, afraid to hope too much. She was talking — the same girl the doctors had warned might never speak again, whose future had been written in scans that showed something blank, silent, unreachable.

Her mother and I stood at the edge of the bed, gripping her hands. We told her. We told her Michael and Meagan were in heaven.

Donna didn't cry. She wasn't confused. She looked at us with a steadiness that didn't belong to a fifteen-year-old girl who had just survived what she survived, and she said, "I know."

Then she said something that changed everything.

"The old life is gone. This is a new life. I saw Jesus, and He said we are to be His disciples."

The room went still. Those words — spoken by a child who had been unconscious for days, who had been pulled from wreckage and revived on an operating table — carried a weight that pressed down on every person standing there. This wasn't confusion. This wasn't medication. This was a message.

The doctor came in — the same one who had shown us the scans, who had told us she might never talk, never feed herself. He looked at her, looked at the monitors, and shook his head. "This ain't the girl we see in the scans. She's not supposed to be talking."

But she was. She was talking, and what she was saying wasn't small talk. It was prophecy.

Even in the joy of that moment, I was overwhelmed. I still didn't know what day it was. I was still the father who had buried two children. But something pierced the darkness — something sharp and bright and undeniable. Donna was awake. She was talking. She was still here. And I felt the unmistakable presence again — the same one from the hospital room with Meagan, the same one that had been hovering over us since the wreck. We were not alone.

"And it shall come to pass afterward, that I will pour out my spirit upon all flesh; and your sons and your daughters shall prophesy, your old men shall dream dreams, your young men shall see visions." — Joel 2:28 KJV

Chapter Seven — Preparing for a Different Life

Donna spent days and weeks in the ICU. Time lost all meaning — morning and night blurred together, measured only by shift changes and the beeping of machines. She spoke, she tried, but nothing was easy. The doctors said she would have to relearn everything.

They gave her a special spoon with a big padded handle so she could try to feed herself. Watching her struggle to lift that spoon — her hand shaking, her face tight with concentration — shattered me in a way I wasn't prepared for. I didn't know if she'd ever walk again. But she was alive. That fragile fact was all we had, and we held on to it with everything we had left.

The reality was this: if Donna came home, nothing would be the same. She would need a wheelchair, wide doorways, open space. And none of us knew if we could walk back into that house. The silence waiting there felt unbearable — the absence of two voices that used to fill every room.

After the doctors said she might come home, I started packing their rooms. We were never wealthy. The house was worn, patched up paycheck to paycheck, held together by sweat and stubbornness. But after the wreck, the community rallied in ways I never expected. People donated. Every dollar went into the house — for Donna.

It wasn't just money, meals, and repairs. It was the way people showed up. Every knock on the door, every envelope pressed into my hand, every stranger who said "I heard what happened and I want to help" — it felt like God reminding us He hadn't left. Their kindness wasn't charity. It was presence. It was proof. It was the hands and feet of Jesus doing what Jesus does.

Before the wreck, Meagan and Donna shared a room. Katie lived with her grandmother at the very house we'd been watching the dogs. Michael had his own room.

Crossing that threshold after the wreck was like stepping into a crypt. The air was cold, unmoving — it echoed with emptiness. No laughter. No feet thudding down the hallway. No one calling "Dad's home!" Just silence, thick and final.

Friends helped me box up the rooms. We started in Michael's. Piece by piece, we gathered his world — his clothes, his toys, the small things that had made his room his. I wept openly, and so did the man beside me. Two grown men, undone by a nine-year-old boy's belongings.

I was kneeling by the window when I noticed it. A rock, sitting on the windowsill. Donna's handiwork — she had always loved rocks, collected them, shaped them, polished them. But this one was different. On one side, carved in her hand: "In God We Trust." On the other side: "Stay Strong."

I froze. The room went hushed. It wasn't just a rock. It was a message — a lifeline sent ahead of the storm, placed there by hands that didn't know what they were preparing for. God had put those words in Donna's heart long before the wreck, and they were sitting on that windowsill waiting for me in my darkest hour.

I felt His presence. Comforting. Reminding. That rock became a promise I could hold in my hand.

"Remember ye not the former things, neither consider the things of old. Behold, I will do a new thing; now it shall spring forth; shall ye not know it? I will even make a way in the wilderness, and rivers in the desert." — Isaiah 43:18-19 KJV

Chapter Eight — The Funeral and the Confirmation

The days before the funeral felt unreal — like moving through water, every step slow and heavy, every decision requiring more strength than I had. My sister and brother-in-law stepped in. They offered to find a dress for Meagan and a suit for Michael. I asked them to find a matching suit for me and Michael — father and son, dressed the same one last time. They did everything with care, with love, with the kind of tenderness that holds a family together when it's falling apart.

Only about five people ever saw Meagan's dress — pink with purple flowers. Michael's suit matched mine. But I later learned they couldn't put the suit on him.

Picking out the coffins was the hardest thing I have ever done. No parent should ever have to stand in a room full of caskets and choose one for their child — let alone two. I stood there, running my hands along the edges, touching the wood, trying to make a decision that no amount of preparation could have readied me for.

Meagan's coffin was covered in roses — soft, delicate, beautiful, just like her. Michael's had four deer, one in each corner. He loved deer. Each man in the family took one of those deer from the corners. I left the last one with him. The funeral director tried to fight me on it — said the deer were too expensive to leave inside the coffin. I didn't care. I told her that's what I wanted, and that was final. Some things you don't compromise on. Not when it's your son. Not when it's the last thing you can give him.

The funeral was Apostolic, held at the church where everyone in the family had been baptized — everyone except Michael and me at the time. That detail weighed on me, heavy with spiritual significance. Donna was still unconscious during the funeral, still fighting for her life in the ICU while we buried her brother and sister.

The procession was unlike anything I had ever seen. People lined the roads. Cars stretched as far as I could see. Teachers, neighbors, friends, strangers — the community came out and honored them in a way that was overwhelming, heartbreaking, and humbling all at once.

After the funeral, after Donna finally woke up, she started talking about seeing them. My wife asked, "Who is it you see?"

Donna said, "Michael and Meagan."

"Where?"

She pointed to the end of her hospital bed. "There."

"What are they wearing?"

Donna answered without hesitating. "Meagan is in a pink dress with purple flowers. And Michael is in pajamas."

Every jaw in that room dropped.

Meagan was buried in that pink dress with purple flowers. Only about five people had ever seen it. And Michael — we believe they placed him in pajamas because they couldn't put the suit on him. Both coffins had been closed. Donna had been unconscious during the entire funeral. No one had described the clothing to her. There is no earthly explanation for how she knew.

This was confirmation. God's presence, God's mercy, showing us that Michael and Meagan were okay — that they were with Him, that they were still near, that the separation we felt was real but not final.

"But I would not have you to be ignorant, brethren, concerning them which are asleep, that ye sorrow not, even as others which have no hope. For if we believe that Jesus died and rose again, even so them also which sleep in Jesus will God bring with him." — 1 Thessalonians 4:13-14 KJV

Chapter Nine — What Donna Saw at the Scene

Some time after Donna and Katie came home, our attorney asked us to meet at the wreck scene. Donna insisted on coming. She was still in a wheelchair, still fragile, still healing, but she needed to be there. She had heard pieces of the story in the hospital, but this was different — she was awake, alert, and on the actual ground where it happened. She needed to show them something.

She didn't hesitate. The moment we arrived, she pointed across the road and told them to take her there. They pushed her chair through the grass. She kept looking around, matching the world with what she had seen.

She lifted her hand and pointed. "He was standing right there."

My wife asked, "Who, baby?"

"Jesus. He was standing right there. But I couldn't see His face."

She said it simply, as a matter of fact — the way a child states something they know to be true without needing anyone to believe them. She couldn't see His face. That lines up with scripture — no man has lived and seen the face of God. Donna didn't know that verse. She wasn't old enough to understand the theology behind it. But what she described matched it perfectly.

Michael and Meagan were there too, she told us. Jesus told Michael he had to come with Him. He gave Meagan a choice — stay with Him or go back. Meagan chose to stay.

That broke me and healed me at the same time. I had always wondered why they revived Meagan at the scene but couldn't stabilize her. Hearing that she was given a choice — and chose to stay with Jesus — made something click into place that I had been struggling to understand.

Then she told us something deeper. Jesus didn't give Donna a choice. He told her she had to go back. And He didn't send her back empty-handed. He sent her with a message — the same words she had spoken the moment she first opened her eyes in the hospital: "The old life is gone. This is a new life. I saw Jesus, and He said we are to be His disciples."

Standing at the scene, hearing her repeat those words with the same certainty she'd had in the hospital bed, something settled in my spirit. This wasn't imagination. It wasn't confusion. It wasn't a child's mind trying to make sense of trauma. It was a message. A calling. Confirmation that God was there before we arrived — with the children, with Donna, with all of us.

She gave great detail that day — pointing, explaining, remembering. She assured us she couldn't see His face, only His presence, only the light. Every word she spoke lined up with scripture, with truth, with things she couldn't have known on her own.

Looking back on the timeline — they revived Meagan but couldn't keep her, Michael never came back, and Donna survived against all medical odds — it all fits together in a way that only God can arrange. Only God can make sense of tragedy.

"We are to be His disciples." Those words have never left me. They still echo in my spirit, still guide me, still remind me that in the darkest moment of my life, God was already there.

"And he said, Thou canst not see my face: for there shall o man see me, and live." — Exodus 33:20 KJV

Chapter Ten — Going Home Without Them

When Donna was released from the hospital, we didn't go straight home. We camped at my mother's house for a few days while the last touches were put on our place. Friends and family had worked hard — fresh paint, new floors, everything scrubbed and redone. But when we finally walked through that door, none of it mattered.

The house wasn't the same. There was a quiet that pushed on your chest — a suffocating silence that reminded you, with every breath, of what was missing. It was sacred and unbearable at once.

There was so much crying. It would crack you open at random — sudden and raw, without warning. You'd be standing in the kitchen or walking past a doorway and a memory would hit you like a fist: a small moment, an everyday thing, a last time you never recognized as an ending. My wife cried until there was nothing left. Grief didn't come in waves. It came like a flood.

I remember her falling asleep in the recliner one night, her face finally peaceful. When she woke, there was a split second — just a heartbeat — when she forgot. And then the truth slammed back in. She screamed, "They're gone!" — like she was hearing it for the first time all over again. The sound of that scream was pure, soul-tearing heartbreak. I will never unhear it.

I slipped into depression. I started drinking, and I drank hard. I didn't care about myself. I didn't care about anything. Grief was physical — it hollowed me out, drained my strength, sat on me like a weight I could never set down. It was a pain that never leaves. You just learn to carry it.

I took my eyes off the Lord for a time. I was angry, broken, lost. But even in my distance, God never took His eyes off me. He was always there, always ahead, always waiting for me to turn back. I feel regret and shame for how far I fell, but I know God caught me. He always catches me.

The years that followed didn't erase the grief. It never left. When tragedy hits, families don't always draw closer. Sometimes the hurt pulls you apart — blame surfaces, each person grieves differently, and no one knows how to bridge the distance that grows between you.

The longing never leaves either — the ache to see them, hold them, hear their voices. Even knowing where they are, knowing they're safe with the Lord, doesn't erase it. It just changes the shape of it.

Going home without them was the start of a new life I never wanted. Every room held a memory. Every silence had a heaviness. Grief became a shadow — a companion never invited but always present. But even in the darkest corners of that house, God was Already There.

Psalm 147:3 (KJV) — "He healeth the broken in heart, and bindeth up their wounds."

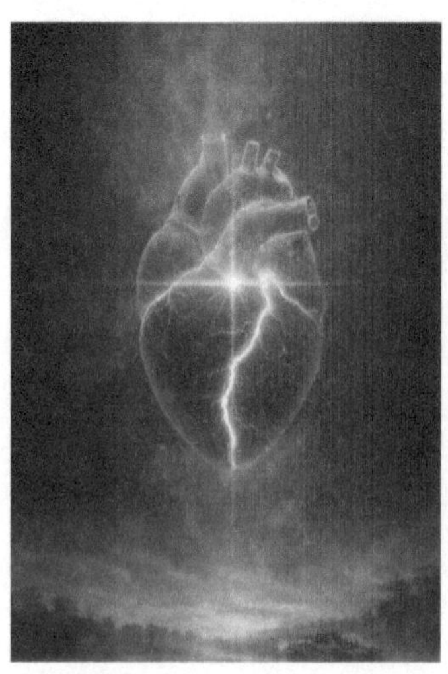

Chapter Eleven — When the World Kept Breaking

Grief doesn't end with the funeral. People think it does — that the burial is the period at the end of the sentence, and after that you start to heal. For us, the funeral was only the beginning of a different kind of pain.

After the funeral, the letters started coming. Kids from school wrote about Michael and Meagan — stories, memories, drawings. Cards arrived from strangers. The community showed up in ways that still humble me. But slowly, people drifted back to their routines. Their lives kept moving. Mine didn't.

Life got hard in ways I didn't expect. The darkness I had fallen into didn't lift — it deepened. Decisions had to be made, big ones, and sometimes nobody had answers. Loneliness crept in even when the house wasn't empty. Fear, anxiety, panic attacks — they became part of daily life, as regular as breathing, as constant as the grief. It got hard to go to work. Maybe because that's where I was when I got the call. Maybe because the last time I left for work, I came home to a world without my kids.

Then there were the tombstones. I ordered them and paid cash. They told me four to six weeks. At week eight, then ten, I started calling. People in the community were asking why the stones weren't there yet. Finally, I drove out there myself. What I found made me sick — they had pushed Michael and Meagan's tombstones to the back of the list because they were working on a tombstone for a movie which was being filmed in Bessemer. A movie prop took priority over two real children. The stones finally came, but they were incomplete.

The water bills were another blow. Not just high — outrageous. Four hundred, five hundred dollars for a single month. I fought them, questioned them, and eventually refused to pay. They pulled the meter. It felt unfair and cruel — life piling on top of grief like it had something personal against us.

We bought property. Our own land, free and clear. But we didn't have enough money for a home. So we lived in a ten-by-twenty storage building, running power off a generator. We made it work. It rained for weeks, and the fresh ground turned to mud. But the water bill was thirty or forty dollars, and the land was ours.

I sold my Kubota tractor and bought a single-wide mobile home. Got power hooked up. Did it all on a five-thousand-dollar budget. It was hard, especially with my wife battling rheumatoid arthritis, ITP, and lupus. My hands were full — all of us still grieving, Donna still recovering, and me terrified of losing the rest of my family every time I walked out the door.

I built a workshop — woodworking equipment, a sawmill. It felt like a step forward, like maybe I could build something again. But people took advantage. I bought logs for a milling business. I was supposed to get several good loads of quality timber. Instead I got one truckload of junk — wood not suitable for the mill. I honored my word and paid two thousand dollars after the first load, even though it wasn't what was agreed. I never received the good logs. Things like that kept happening — people seeing a grieving man and seeing an opportunity.

The world kept testing us, stretching us, pushing us to the edge. Through it all, we kept going. Not because we were strong. Not because we had answers. Because there was no other choice.

This was the part no one saw. After the flowers wilted and the casseroles stopped coming. Life didn't just hurt — it demanded everything we had left.

"And we know that all things work together for good to them that love God, to them who are the called according to his purpose." — Romans 8:28 KJV

Chapter Twelve — Not Today

COVID came and the world shut down. For most people, it was unprecedented. For us, it was another blow in a long line of them. We kept food in the house and kept our heads down.

Then the power bill problem started. At first I thought it was a mistake. My sawmill was gas-powered — it wasn't pulling electricity. But the bills kept climbing. Eight hundred dollars. A thousand. Twelve hundred. Month after month, the numbers made no sense.

I started running the shop entirely on the generator to prove something wasn't right. I called the power company over and over. Same answer every time: "That's your bill. Pay it."

One morning, I woke with a sinking feeling — this is the day they disconnect. I got on my knees and prayed. And I heard my Father's voice in my spirit, as clear as anything I've ever heard: "Not today."

I went out to cut wood. I was at the sawmill, straining to turn a log by hand, when the power company man pulled up. I walked over to him and said, "I know what you have to do. I don't blame you. But something isn't right with these bills."

He looked at his disconnect order, then looked back at me. "You're right. Something isn't right. These addresses don't match."

The meter was registered in Fultondale but was being used at my house. The day it was installed, the man had asked if I wanted a new meter, and I said sure. He grabbed one from the back of his truck. That meter had its own story — it carried charges from an address that wasn't mine.

The disconnect man said the same words I'd heard in prayer: "Not today." Then he added, "I'm hiding this work order in my truck. I can't seem to find it." He was listening to the Father too.

I called the power company again — same argument, same wall. Nobody would listen. "Pay your bill."

Within a few days, I had to sell my wife's car to keep the power on. The bill was twenty-eight hundred dollars. Losing that car meant losing her independence — we couldn't afford to replace it. But we did what we had to do.

That bought us three months. Then they disconnected us anyway.

No more answers. I needed my table saw to finish a customer's swings, but the generator was worn out. Donna and I prayed over that saw. I told her, "I know it won't run, but I hear the Lord telling me to call the power company."

I called at six in the evening. I fought for twenty minutes, pushing through the same resistance, the same scripted answers. Finally they put me through to a supervisor. Everything changed.

She asked for my Social Security number and the meter numbers. Something so simple — something no one had ever asked for before.

Then — boom.

"Sir, I'll call you back in thirty minutes." She called back in less than five. "Sir, I'm sending someone out to turn your power back on now." After hours. That never happens.

I knew. God was in this.

The next morning, the same lady called. She told me they were issuing a credit for roughly four thousand dollars. I asked if any of it could be refunded in cash. She said no — it wasn't possible.

Two days later, she called again. They had found an additional four hundred and fifty dollars and could send it as cash.

For the first time in months, the bills were normal — two to three hundred dollars. But the damage was done. My wife's car was gone. Her independence was gone. We were still climbing out of a hole we never should have been pushed into.

Even in all that loss, all that unfairness, all that exhaustion — God still whispered: Not today.

"I shall not die, but live, and declare the works of the LORD." — Psalm 118:17 KJV

Chapter Thirteen — When the Cracks Became Canyons

Grief breaks a family slowly, over years, in ways you don't see until the damage is done.

My wife started to withdraw. She stayed home more and more. Her flare-ups were getting worse — there were days she couldn't move, couldn't get out of bed. I stayed home to care for her, but staying home had a cost. I couldn't keep everything under control. There were too many fires, too many problems, too many things breaking at once.

We were living on disability income — less than nine hundred dollars a month. That was supposed to cover everything. Then the Biden years came and prices shot up. Inflation hit like a hammer. Shop orders barely covered supplies. By the time I bought parts, there was almost nothing left for profit. The power bill was climbing again.

Donna wanted to learn to drive. The same girl the doctors said might never feed herself — now she wanted to get behind the wheel. She's a fighter, always has been. But I was nervous. We only had one vehicle — my truck.

I was in the passenger seat when someone pulled out in front of us. Donna froze. Confusion hit her, and she slammed into a steel pole sign at forty-five miles per hour. The front end caved in, stopped half an inch from the radiator. It was a miracle I could even drive it home. My neighbor and I pulled the front end back out. Donna kept learning.

It happened again. My wife and Donna were on the way to take her to work. I heard a beeping sound from outside — like a truck backing up. I looked out the window and saw my truck on a wrecker. Both right-side rims were crushed. Donna had run off the road and hit a boulder.

No vehicle. No way to get supplies, get to work, get anywhere. We sat without a vehicle for over a month. Couldn't afford new rims. Then found out the rear axle was broken. A neighbor took me to the store for food. Family was nowhere to be found. We were secluded. Forgotten. It felt like nobody cared. It was awful.

The only thing I could do was pray.

I got the truck running again. But the damage to the family was deepening. Grief was cutting deeper than ever. We couldn't catch a break. Every time we stood up, life knocked us back down.

My wife and I started drifting apart. It wasn't her fault. It wasn't mine either. The stress of everything — the grief, the poverty, the constant crises — it crushes marriages. It crushes hope. It crushes the parts of you that used to feel strong. There was no winning. Everything was hard. Some people took their eyes off God. Some found other gods to fill the void. My faith held. After everything I had witnessed — the miracles, the messages, the moments when God showed up in ways that defied explanation — I couldn't walk away from Him. But even faith doesn't erase the weight of living.

Eventually the day came. My wife left. One final kiss. One final "I love you." And then the words that ended everything: "I can't keep living like this." For the first time in these pages, I'll call her my ex-wife. We divorced. We sold the home and the property.

There is so much darkness in those years — not in the memories of my children, which still shine, but in everything that followed. It all fell apart. Grief turned to survival. Survival turned to exhaustion.

I'm not glad about the divorce. But I'm glad that place is gone — the place where the rest of my life fell apart. Sometimes you have to leave the ruins behind to hope for a future.

"And he said unto me, My grace is sufficient for thee: for my strength is made perfect in weakness." — 2 Corinthians 12:9 KJV

Chapter Fourteen — Already There

Sometimes I go back in my mind to the little rock on the windowsill. It showed up long before the wreck, long before the grief, long before the losses that would follow for years. I didn't know then what I know now. The words carved into that stone — "In God We Trust" and "Stay Strong" — felt simple at the time. Now I know they were a warning, a promise, and a lifeline, all at once. God was preparing me for a storm I couldn't see coming.

It's been seven years. Seven years of loss, rebuilding, and learning to breathe again.

Through it all, I have remained a God-fearing man. Not because I'm strong. Not because I'm perfect. But because I've seen too much of what my Father can do to ever walk away.

I know God gave me this testimony for a reason — a purpose bigger than my pain. I don't know exactly where I'm going, but I know this: God is Already There.

I can see His hand in places I once thought were empty. His presence in moments I thought I'd been abandoned. His purpose in seasons I thought were meaningless.

God has given me something new — a grandchild. And another on the way. I know she's going to be a girl. A reminder that life continues. Beauty from ashes. The story isn't over.

I have to trust Him. I have to stay strong. He hasn't brought me this far to leave me now.

God brings people into your life in ways too perfectly orchestrated to be coincidence. Too precise to be chance. Too meaningful to be random. When God moves, He moves with intention.

I know deep in my spirit that my Father in heaven wants this story told. He trusted me with this testimony for a reason. Maybe that reason is you.

Who do you worship? What faith do you carry? What would you do if your world fell apart? Where would you go when everything you love is gone?

Here is what I learned in the darkest places a man can walk: He's Already There. He hasn't forgotten you. He hasn't abandoned you. He hasn't turned His face away.

He hasn't missed a single tear. He hasn't lost track of your pain. He hasn't stopped working on your behalf.

"Whither shall I go from thy spirit? or whither shall I flee from thy presence? If I ascend up into heaven, thou art there: if I make my bed in hell, behold, thou art there." — Psalm 139:7-8 KJV

"God is our refuge and strength, a very present help in trouble." — Psalm 46:1 KJV

"That they should seek the Lord, if haply they might feel after him, and find him, though he be not far from every one of us." — Acts 17:27 KJV

This is not the end of my story. It is the beginning of understanding why I survived it. And if you're reading this — maybe it's the beginning of yours too.

"And the LORD, he it is that doth go before thee; he will be with thee, he will not fail thee, neither forsake thee: fear not, neither be dismayed." — Deuteronomy 31:8 KJV

Closing Prayer

Father, I come before You with a heart that has been broken, rebuilt, stretched, and carried by Your hands. You have walked with me through fire, through loss, through fear, through loneliness, and through every valley I never wanted to enter. And yet, You never left me. Not once.

Thank You for the strength You gave me when I had none.
Thank You for the moments when Your voice broke through the darkness.
Thank You for the miracles I didn't deserve but desperately needed.
Thank You for the love of my children, the memories that still breathe, and the promise that I will see them again.

Lord, use this testimony for Your glory.
Let these words reach the one who needs them most.
Let this story be a reminder that You are close to the brokenhearted,
that You bind up wounds no one else can see,
and that You are already in every tomorrow we fear.

Father, guide my steps from here.

Lead me into the purpose You prepared long before I was born.

And let my life — even the shattered pieces — point back to You.

In Jesus' name,

Amen.

A Letter to Michael and Meagan

My sweet Michael and my beautiful Meagan,

There isn't a day that passes that I don't think of you. Not one.

Your laughter, your voices, your presence — they still live in me.

You changed my life in ways I never understood until you were gone.

I want you both to know something:

I have carried you with me through every chapter of this story.
 Every struggle. Every prayer. Every moment I wanted to give up. You were there.

Michael, my boy — you were strong, brave, and full of heart.
 I still see your smile. I still hear your footsteps.
 I still feel the weight of the deer I left with you — a symbol of the men who loved you and the man you were becoming.

Meagan, my girl — gentle, kind, full of light.
 Your roses were perfect for you.
 You brought beauty into every room you walked into,
and you still do.
 Your spirit has never stopped blooming in my heart.

I want you both to know that your story didn't end the
day you left this world.
 You live on in every word of this book.
 You live on in every person who reads it.
 You live on in the strength God gave me to survive what
should have destroyed me.

I miss you more than words can hold.
 But I know — I know — I will see you again.

And until that day, I will keep telling your story.
 I will keep honoring your lives.
 I will keep trusting the God who holds you now.

I love you both,
 Dad

Dedication

This book is dedicated to Michael and Meagan —

 my children, my heart, my greatest blessings.

Your lives changed mine forever, and your love

continues to guide me.

 Every page of this testimony carries your fingerprints.

 Every chapter carries your memory.

 Every word carries the love a father never stops giving.

To Anne Stuart Baldwin —

 thank you for taking me in when I had nowhere to go,

 for giving me shelter,

 and for feeding me when I was hungry.

 Your kindness was a lifeline in a season when I had

nothing left.

 You showed me the love of Christ in action,

 and I will never forget what you did for me.

To Dianne Cooper —

 thank you for being part of my future,

 for walking into my life at a time when God knew I

needed someone,

 and for reminding me that new chapters are still

possible.

Your presence is a gift I didn't expect but deeply cherish.

And to anyone walking through darkness, loss, fear, or the unknown —

may you discover what I learned the hardest way a man can learn it:

God is Already There.

The Already There Project

The Already There Project was born from loss, rebuilt through faith, and carried forward by the unshakable truth that God is present long before we arrive at our darkest moments. This project exists to honor the lives of Michael and Meagan, to share the testimony God entrusted to me, and to reach anyone who feels alone, forgotten, or overwhelmed by the weight of their own story.

This is more than a book. It is a reminder. A message. A calling.

God is already in your tomorrow. Already in your healing. Already in your restoration. Already in the place you fear to walk.

If this testimony has touched your heart, if it has stirred something inside you, if it has reminded you that you are not walking alone — then The Already There Project has fulfilled its purpose.

My prayer is that this story becomes a light for those still searching for hope, a comfort for those who are grieving, and a reminder for those who feel forgotten that the Father has never left their side.

This project will continue — through words, through music, through testimony, through every door God opens. And wherever it goes, it carries one message:

He was there in the beginning.
 He is here now.
 And He is already waiting for you in every step ahead.

Thank you for reading my story.
 Thank you for carrying it with you.
 And may God meet you exactly where you are —
 because He is Already There.

Visit the Project Online

www.TheAlreadyThereProject.com

Or on Facebook as Brian Scoggins

Scripture quotations are from the King James Version (KJV).

ISBN 979-8-9956508-0-5

Printed in the United States of America